GOD'S BIG PROMISES
The First Christmas

Over **60** reusable stickers

thegoodbook for children

God's Big Promises The First Christmas Sticker Book | © The Good Book Company 2023

thegoodbook.com | thegoodbook.co.uk | thegoodbook.com.au | thegoodbook.co.nz | thegoodbook.co.in

Written by Carl Laferton | Illustrations by Jennifer Davison | Design and Art Direction by André Parker

ISBN: 9781784989002 | JOB-007288 | Printed in Turkey

God Promises a Special Baby

For hundreds of years, God made huuuuuge promises to his people. He promised King David that one day, someone in his family would be a king who ruled forever. He promised one of his messengers, Isaiah, that he would send someone to rescue his people. He promised another messenger, Micah, that this special king would be born in a town called Bethlehem.

Match the person Go
gave the promise t
with the promis

A rescuing king

Born in Bethlehem

A forever king

Trace the words to finish the sentence:

God made lots of promises about a special baby

Circle words starting with the same letter as the word "promise".

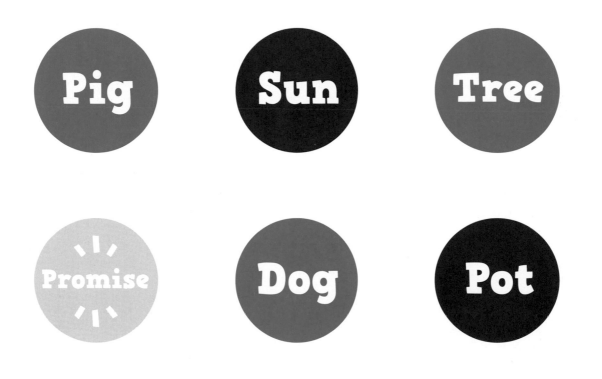

Pig Sun Tree

Promise Dog Pot

So, for years and years and years and years, God's people asked, "When will this special baby be born? What will he be like? What will his name be?"

An Angel Visits Mary

Hundreds of years had passed since God had made his promises to his people. Then, one day, he sent an angel to a little town called Nazareth and to a young woman called Mary.

The angel was named Gabriel, and here was his message:
"Mary, you are going to have a..."

"Your baby will be God's Son, he will be the king of God's people, and he will rule forever," Gabriel told Mary.

Mary was very surprised!
Find the speech-bubble stickers
to read what she said.

You can read all about this in the Bible, in Luke chapter 1 verses 26 to 38

The Angel Speaks to Joseph

Mary was planning to marry Joseph. When Joseph found out that Mary was having a baby and he was not the baby's father, he decided he didn't want to marry Mary anymore.

The angel Gabriel told Joseph to marry Mary, because the baby was God's Son. "Call him Jesus," Gabriel said, "because he will rescue his people."

Joseph and Mary both came from the family of King David. Stick in the stickers, and then find the path that leads from David to Joseph.

Use the code down the side to find out what this sentence says.

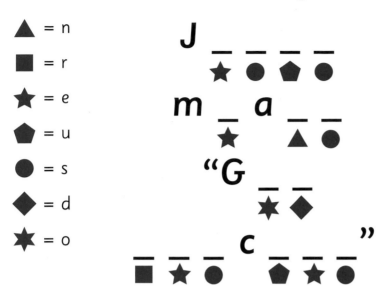

▲ = n
■ = r
★ = e
⬟ = u
● = s
◆ = d
✶ = o

Mary and Joseph were married. Mary felt so happy about her baby that she sang a thank-you song about God.

God is amazing! I'm so happy because God is my rescuer, he cares for me!

Read all about this in Matthew 1 v 18-25 and Luke 1 v 46-55

Jesus Is Born

The Roman emperor wanted to count the people he ruled over. Even though Mary was about to have her baby, Mary and Joseph had to travel to Bethlehem.

Find the path for Mary and Joseph to get to Bethlehem:

GOD'S **BIG** PROMISES

The First Christmas

I am God's servant.

I am ready for all this to happen.

Promise

?

In Bethlehem, Mary's baby was born. She named him Jesus. Because there was nowhere else for him to sleep, Mary wrapped Jesus in cloths and put him in a manger, where animal food was kept.

Read all about this in Luke 2 v 1-7

The Shepherds Find Baby Jesus

In some fields nearby, some shepherds were looking after their sheep. It was a dark night... and then suddenly everything was bright light... and an angel was there!

The shepherds were very scared!

Finish this picture by drawing some angels

"I have good news that will make you very happy," the angel said. "A baby has just been born. He will be your rescuer. He is your king. He is lying in a manger in Bethlehem."

When the angel had gone, the shepherds hurried to Bethlehem. They found the baby Jesus in the manger, just as the angel had said.

Can you spot six differences?

The shepherds weren't scared anymore. Now, they were full of joy and full of praise to God.

Draw *the face of one of the* shepherds, showing how he felt.

Read all about this in Luke 2 v 8-20

Simeon and Anna Meet Jesus

Joseph and Mary took baby Jesus to Jerusalem. They wanted to visit the temple to say thank you to God for him.

In Jerusalem lived an old, old man named Simeon and an old, old woman named Anna. God showed them both who Jesus is.

When he saw Jesus, Simeon said, "God, you have kept your promise. I am looking at the way you will rescue your people and bring joy to people all over the world."

Trace what Simeon and Anna said when they met Jesus:

Thank you God!

Find these words from the story in the wordsearch:

c	s	i	m	e	o	n	p
r	f	s	a	k	n	t	u
m	s	j	r	o	n	j	s
p	r	o	m	i	s	e	h
b	a	y	i	r	x	s	p
o	n	t	a	e	c	u	o
d	n	a	d	y	u	s	a
j	a	e	r	q	t	u	t

☐ Simeon
☐ Anna
☐ Jesus
☐ joy
☐ promise

Read all about this in Luke 2 v 22-38

The Wise Men Follow a Star

Some wise men who lived a long, long way away saw a new star in the sky. They knew that it meant God's promise-keeping king had been born. So they decided to go and find him.

Can you help the wise men find the way to Bethlehem by following the star?

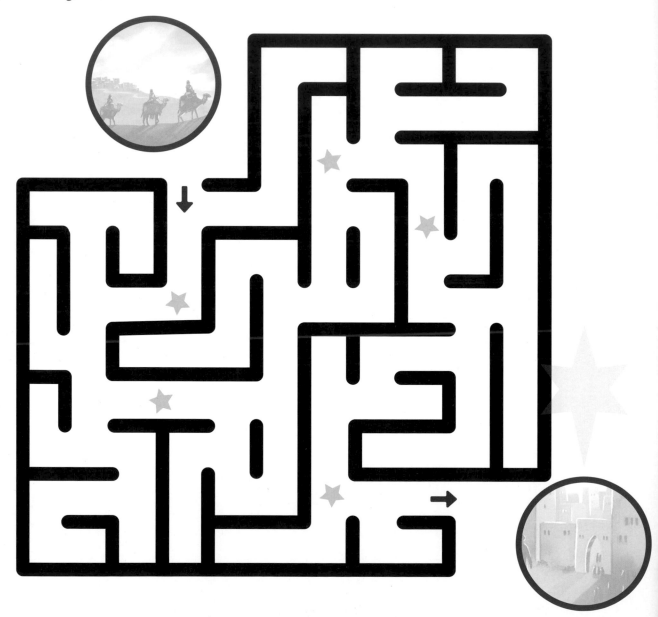

Use the dot to dot to draw the star for the wise men to follow...

When they found the place where Jesus was, the wise men bowed down to him and gave him presents: gold, frankincense and myrrh. They had found God's rescuing, forever king!

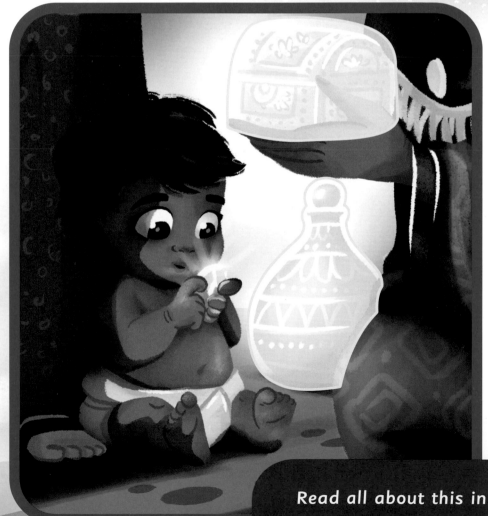

Read all about this in Matthew 2 v 1-2 & 9-11

Happy Christmas

Can you find the stickers and put them in the right order to tell the story of the first Christmas?

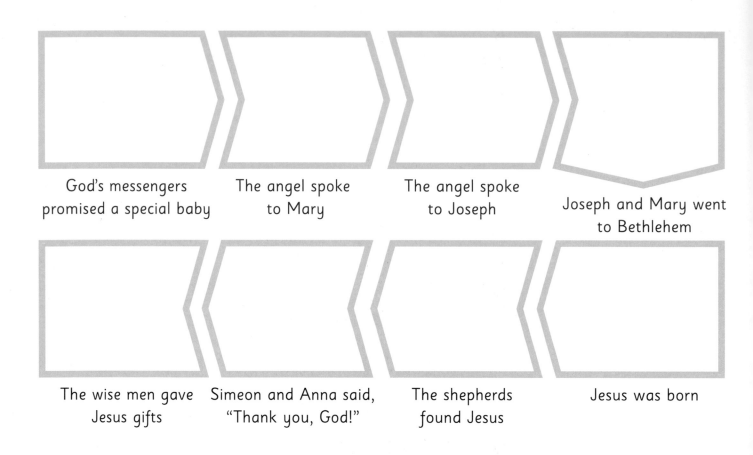

God's messengers promised a special baby

The angel spoke to Mary

The angel spoke to Joseph

Joseph and Mary went to Bethlehem

The wise men gave Jesus gifts

Simeon and Anna said, "Thank you, God!"

The shepherds found Jesus

Jesus was born

Trace the words to remember why Jesus being born is the best news ever:

Jesus is our king and he is our rescuer